Louis and Zélie Martin

Saints of Matrimony

Louis Martin
1823-1894
Born in Bordeaux, France
Marie-Azélie "Zélie" Guérin Martin
1831-1877
Born in Gandelain, France
Feast Day: July 12

Text by Barbara Yoffie
Illustrated by Jeff Albrecht

Dedication

To my family:
my parents Jim and Peg,
my husband Bill,
our son Sam and daughter-in-law Erin,
and our precious grandchildren
Ben, Lucas, and Andrew

To all the children I have had the privilege
of teaching throughout the years.

Imprimi Potest:
Stephen T. Rehrauer, CSsR, Provincial
Denver Province, the Redemptorists

Imprimatur:
In accordance with CIC 827, permission to publish has been granted on April 12, 2018, by the Most Reverend Mark S. Rivituso, Auxiliary Bishop, Archdiocese of St. Louis. Permission to publish is an indication that nothing contrary to Church teaching is contained in this work. It does not imply any endorsement of the opinions expressed in the publication; nor is any liability assumed by this permission.

Published by Liguori Publications, Liguori, Missouri 63057

To order, visit Liguori.org or call 800-325-9521.

ISBN 978-0-7648-2794-5

Liguori Publications, a nonprofit corporation, is an apostolate of the Redemptorists. To learn more about the Redemptorists, visit Redemptorists.com.

Printed in the United States of America
22 21 20 19 18 / 5 4 3 2 1
First Edition

Dear Parents and Teachers:

Saints and Me! is a series of children's books about saints, with six books apiece in the first four sets. The first set, *Saints of North America,* honors holy men and women who blessed and served the land we call home. The second, *Saints of Christmas*, includes heavenly heroes who inspire us through Advent and Christmas and teach us to love the Infant Jesus. The third, *Saints for Families*, introduces saints who modeled God's love within and for the domestic Church. The fourth, *Saints for Communities,* explores individuals from different times and places who served Jesus through their various roles and professions.

The seven books in the *Saints for Sacraments* series explore eight saints who had great love for the sacraments. John the Baptist baptized Jesus in the Jordan River. Padre Pio helped people make a good confession. Teresa of Ávila was known for her great love of the Eucharist. Philip Neri received the Holy Spirit after praying to God. Louis and Zélie Martin, a married couple, taught their children to serve God and the poor. At an early age, John Vianney wanted to dedicate his life to God as a priest; today he is the patron saint of parish priests. Maximilian Kolbe battled poor health to become a priest and brought God's healing to sick people.

Name the saint who lived in the desert and ate locusts and honey. In this set of books, who was the saint with stigmata? Who began a Carmelite convent dedicated to prayer? Who grew up during the French Revolution? Which saints were the parents of Thérèse of Lisieux? Who volunteered to die in place of a stranger in a prison camp? Find out in the *Saints for Sacraments* set—part of the *Saints and Me!* series—and help children connect to the lives of the saints.

Introduce your children or students to the *Saints and Me!* series as they:

—**READ** about the lives of the saints and are inspired by their stories.

—**PRAY** to the saints for their intercession.

—**CELEBRATE** the saints and relate them to their lives.

Saints for Sacraments

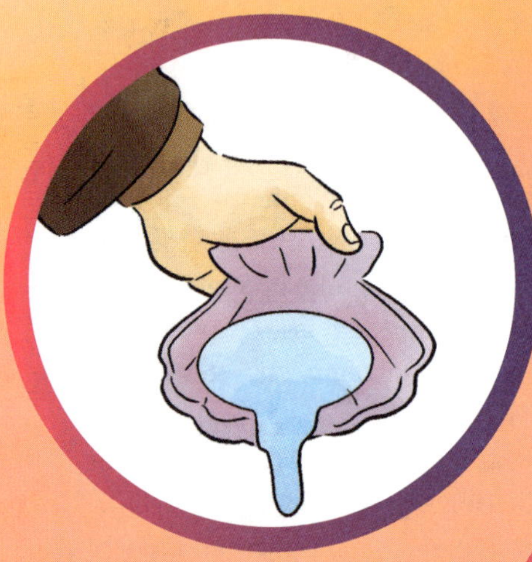

John the Baptist
Baptism

Teresa of Ávila
Eucharist

Philip Neri
Confirmation

Padre Pio
Reconciliation

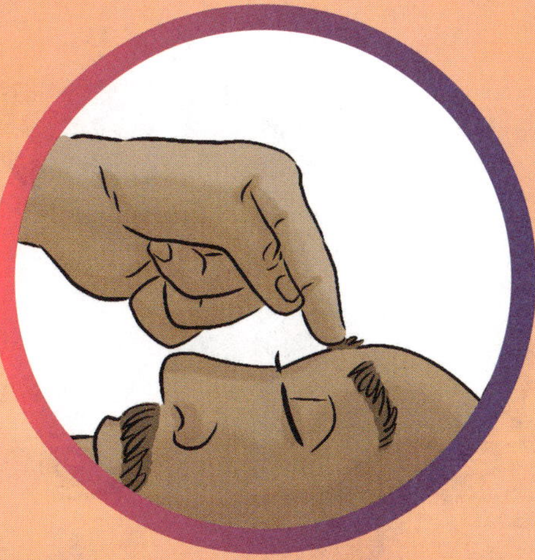

Maximilian Kolbe
Anointing of the Sick

Louis and Zélie Martin
Matrimony

John Vianney
Holy Orders

Louis and Zélie Martin are two special saints. They are the first married couple to be canonized together. Marriage is a vocation, a special calling from God to live a holy life. Louis and Zélie loved God very much. God blessed their marriage and helped them to grow in holiness.

Louis was a quiet little boy who lived in Alençon, France. He liked to play outside. He liked to hike and fish. His parents taught Louis all about God. They taught him how to pray. "God is always with you," said his mother.

When Louis grew up, he wanted to join the monastery. Here he could pray and grow closer to God. But he could not join the monastery. God had a different plan for Louis. In a few years he would understand. Louis became a watchmaker. He opened a watchmaking shop in the peaceful town of Alençon.
FINE LACE

Zélie's family moved to Alençon when she was thirteen years old. Her older sister entered the convent. Zélie wanted to become a nun, too, but was turned away because of her health. "God must want me to marry and have children," Zélie decided. She learned how to make very beautiful lace. Smart and hard-working, Zélie started her own lace-making business.

CLOCKS

One day, Louis and Zélie were both crossing the St. Leonard Bridge in Alençon. Zélie saw Louis. Louis saw Zélie. They met, fell in love, and soon married. Louis and Zélie Martin loved each other very much. They shared their faith and their great love of God. They prayed together and shared their dreams for the future.

"I think God brought us together," Louis told Zélie. "I think you are right, Louis." In the sacrament of marriage, a husband and wife promise to love each other forever. A married couple grows in faith and holiness together. They are faithful to each other and respect one another.

One of their dreams came true when their first baby was born. They named her Marie. “She is a precious gift from God,” Louis said. The Martins were so happy. They were blessed with four more daughters who lived to adulthood. Each baby brought them great joy.

Life was busy for the Martin family raising five daughters, Marie, Pauline, Léonie, Céline, and little Thérèse. They loved to spend time in the country hiking and playing in the garden. In the evening, they sat near the fireplace and read stories. They all enjoyed singing. The two youngest, Céline and Thérèse, would sit on Louis' lap. "Please, Papa, sing another song," they cried. After prayers and a kiss good night, it was time for bed.

The Martin home was full of faith, love, and joy. “Our children make us so happy,” Zélie told her friends. Zélie taught the girls to do small things to make Jesus happy. They shared their faith by word and example. The day would begin with prayer and Mass. Louis and Zélie both worked very hard but still took time to visit the sick and help the poor. They raised their children to love God and help others. These were lessons the girls would always remember.

Thérèse was only four when Zélie became very ill. Doctors could not help her. Sadness filled their home. Louis and Zélie always took care of each other, but now they would be apart. Zélie died peacefully with Louis at her bedside.

Louis moved his family to the town of Lisieux. He bought a house with a garden at the edge of the town. Now they lived close to their Uncle Isidore, Aunt Céline, and their cousins. Living near family was a great comfort. Louis raised his daughters with great love and patience.

After a few years, Pauline, then Marie, joined the Carmelite convent and became nuns. Léonie entered the Visitation convent. Louis knew God was calling them, and that made him very happy. Zélie had always prayed that the girls might become nuns.

Shortly after Thérèse entered the Carmelite convent at the young age of fifteen, Louis became ill. It was hard for him to remember things. He stayed at a hospital for a long time. Even when Louis was sick he was thankful for everything God had given him. After three years he returned home. Céline took care of him until he died. She wrote her sisters, “Papa is in heaven.” Then it was time for Céline to enter the convent, too.

Louis and Zélie Martin always put God first. In happy and sad times, God was with them. They are wonderful examples of joy in married life, holy parenthood, and raising faith-filled children who were called to be saints.

Their youngest daughter, Saint Thérèse of Lisieux, also known as the "Little Flower," was canonized in 1925. In 2015, a cause for canonization was opened for Léonie (Sister Françoise-Thérèse).

A family blessed with faith and love
is a great gift from God above.

Saints Louis and Zélie,
you loved God
and you loved each other
very much.
Your children filled you
with joy
and happiness.
You shared your faith
and your holiness.
Help my family to become
holy like yours.
Amen.

GLOSSARY (NEW WORDS)

Alençon: A town in northwestern France that was famous for its lace since the seventeenth century

Canonize: To name someone a saint

Carmelite: A religious order founded in the twelfth century whose nuns dedicate themselves to prayer and sacrifice

Convent: A house where a group of women religious live

Lisieux: A town in northwestern France, about fifty miles north of Alençon

Monastery: The place where a religious order of men lives, prays, and works

Sacraments: The seven special signs of God's life and love

Visitation: A religious order founded in 1610 by Saint Francis de Sales and Saint Jane Frances de Chantal

Vocation: A call from God to serve him in a special way